CASTLE DROGO

Devon

THE NATIONAL TRUST

Castle Drogo is four miles south of the A30 Exeter–Okehampton road via Crockernwell.

As far as possible Castle Drogo is today presented to resemble the family home that Julius Drewe would recognise. Restraints on visitors wishing to walk around the house have been kept to a minimum. Nevertheless, the National Trust would be failing in its primary duty of preservation if some precautions were not taken to prevent unacceptable deterioration of the house and its furnishings. Thus the prohibition of stiletto heels, the occasional rope barrier and carpet druggets are used to protect floors and carpets. Light, too, is restricted by the use of blinds and sun curtains, and ultraviolet filters are applied to the windows to prevent irreversible damage to textiles, paintings and furniture. Visitors are also asked not to touch objects in the rooms. For reasons of conservation and security and to avoid inconvenience to other visitors, photography inside the castle is not allowed.

Hugh Meller, 1995

Photographs: Robert Chapman pp. 44, 45; Devon County Record Office p. 27; Peter Inskip p. 43; National Trust pp. 39, 41, 42; NT/Jon Hicks front cover; National Trust Photographic Library pp. 26, 40; NTPL/ Neil Campbell-Sharp pp. 28, 29, 31; NTPL/T. Davidson p. 33; NTPL/Chris Gascoigne p. 47; NTPL/John Hammond pp. 12, 18, 25, 36, 37, 38; NTPL/Angelo Hornak pp. 4, 7, 30; NTPL/ James Mortimer pp. 1, 5, 10, 11, 13, 15, 16, 17, 20, 21, 22, 23, 24, 48, back cover.

First published in 1995 by the National Trust
© 1995 The National Trust
Registered charity no. 205846
Revised 1996, 1999, 2003, 2005 Reprinted 1998, 2000, 2002

ISBN 1 84359 0646

Designed by James Shurmer

Phototypeset in Monotype Bembo Series 270 by Intraspan Limited, Smallfield, Surrey (SG1664)

Print managed by Astron for the National Trust (Enterprises) Ltd, 36 Queen Anne's Gate, London SW1H 9AS

CONTENTS

The castle from the south-east; watercolour by Cyril Farey, 1923 (acquired with help from the National Art Collections Fund)

INTRODUCTION

CASTLE DROGO is the creation of two men: Julius Drewe, the founder of the Home and Colonial Stores, who had the means and inspiration to commission the house; and Edwin Lutyens, his architect, whose unique design combines the austerity of a medieval castle with the comforts of a family home.

Julius Drewe (1856–1931) retired from business in 1889 a rich man, and for some while lived in Sussex before buying the Drogo Estate in Drewsteignton in 1910. During the intervening years he had researched his ancestry and assumed a relationship with a Norman baron, Drogo de Teign, after whom the parish of Drewsteignton had been named in the twelfth century. Visions of ancient family roots sparked his imagination, encouraged further by panoramic vistas of Dartmoor viewed from his newly acquired land. A spectacular building, a castle, was demanded to satisfy his dream of an ancestral home.

Drewe's choice of architect was equally inspired: Edwin Lutyens (1869–1944), the greatest of English twentieth-century architects, was in his prime and undaunted by either his determined client or his unusual brief. His preliminary sketches envisaged a house of heroic size, but practicalities and the intervention of the First World War prevailed and the size was gradually reduced by about two-thirds. Nevertheless, the surviving granite wing is impressive enough and took 20 years to build. It is complemented by formal gardens on three terraced levels to the north-east, which Lutyens also helped to design.

Julius Drewe died having lived only a few years in his new home. He was succeeded by his son Basil, and in 1974 by his grandson Anthony, who continued to live in the castle. It was Anthony Drewe and his son Christopher who gave the house and 600 acres to the National Trust in 1974, the first twentieth-century house to pass into its possession.

Mr Drewe's Room

CHAPTER ONE

THE EXTERIOR

All the roads to Castle Drogo are high-banked, narrow Devon lanes, so it comes as a surprise, and increases the sense of anticipation, when unexpectedly the lanes open into a *rond-point* within clipped beech hedges, and the broad drive to Castle Drogo rises steadily to the south-east. It was here, in 1910, that Mrs Drewe pulled up a mangold from the field as a symbolic gesture to mark the start of the drive, bordered for half a mile by unfenced grass verges, bracken and trees, and curving westwards to reveal a glorious view of Dartmoor. The effect is stunning and credit for the idea is due to Julius Drewe, who in 1915 wrote to Lutyens, 'So far as the Drive is concerned . . . what I want is heather, bracken, broom, holly, brambles, foxgloves, etc.' Lutyens agreed and suggested the scheme should be laid 'before Miss Jekyll who is a great designer and Artist, old and experienced in the way of plants and a lover of the Wilderness and of moorland'. Gertrude Jekyll was also a long-standing friend of Lutyens (who addressed her as 'Your Bumpship' when he wrote to her about the Drogo project a few days later). Although in her seventies and almost blind, she produced a planting scheme; in addition to wild flowers she introduced circles of ilex at the *rond-point* and curve and also the pair of yew hedges through which the drive still passes. These are the only formal accents, although there were once plans to link the hedges to a pair of cottages and to add a pair of curious triangular-shaped lodges at the curve.

From that curve the drive continues another half-mile on the only easily accessible route to the castle, which stands alone on a rocky outcrop. The first glimpse of the narrow north-east façade is unflattering but through no fault of Lutyens, who had cherished ambitions for a more spectacular approach – a mighty barbican comprising a four-storey gate-tower between corbelled bastions linking the two sides of the ridge. He went so far as to build a full-scale timber and tarpaulin mock-up to persuade his client, but it was not to be. Yew hedges were planted instead and after 50 years these have grown into passable substitutes. Also incomplete were south and west wings to the house, which had been planned in 1911 and would have tripled its size. The foundations were built but in 1912 plans changed and work on them stopped, leaving only the generous expanse of forecourt as their testimony.

Before reaching the main entrance on the west flank, visitors must pass the gloomily austere North Tower, lit by a few small windows cut deep into the solid granite masonry. The tower acted as a service wing but the impression is convincingly medieval and military on account of the crenellations and complete lack of guttering, downpipes, window drip-moulds and sills. The lower curtain wall that follows shields the top lighting of the larders and the kitchen behind it, with, between them, a projecting bathroom wing. Then, beyond that wall there is a jump in style, from the medieval to the Tudor, and with it a jump in scale; everything becomes larger, especially the mullioned and transomed windows, indicating the more spacious family living-quarters within.

The entrance tower is the focus: the octagonal turrets are the highest points of the castle and the only exterior decoration is the heraldic Drewe lion. This was carved by Herbert Palliser (1883–1963), a Yorkshireman then teaching at the Royal College of Art, who added beneath it the Drewe motto *Drogo Nomen et Virtus Arma Dedit* ('Drewe is the name and valour gave it arms'). He was already known to Lutyens, having carved two lions for the architect's war memorial in Richmond, South Africa (1920).

Two other aspects of Lutyens's architecture are

The castle from the west; watercolour by Cyril Farey, 1924 (acquired with help from the National Art Collections Fund)

demonstrated by this tower: his subtle attention to detail and his sense of fun. The detail occurs in his skilful use of battering – the technique of inclining the face of a wall. He did this throughout the castle, particularly in the east elevation, but here he used it not once but twice. Thus the tower batters at the base, then rises vertically before battering again above the ground floor. An increased sensation of height is the result. The fun appears in the teeth of the portcullis which grins above the entrance arch. Incredibly this is no sham but a 644lb working example which was operated by a winch in one of the turrets.

Beyond the tower and towards the short south front Lutyens's confidence seems to grow. Here the land falls away but the level of the parapet never falters, with impressive results. The battered walls of the front rest on large rocks, giving every impression of a natural feature. In fact the rocks were moved here in 1912 with the aid of a notoriously

unstable sheerlegs crane that caused a number of accidents. The flat plane of the wall is mainly filled by mullioned windows, but as the wall rises to the second floor, acutely angled wings, like vertical fins, emerge each side. The effect is as startling as it is original, and a virtuoso performance of the mason's craft.

To the west, the apse of the Chapel juts into the moorland. To the east, the wall follows a precipitous line past the main staircase bay, pierced by a cathedral-sized window, to the Library bay. Then there is a change in axis to the more modest north wing, which housed offices, family bedrooms and nurseries. The wall seems to undulate between the two three-storey projecting bays, each punctuated by bands of windows, a device Lutyens used many times in his larger houses.

PLANS OF THE HOUSE

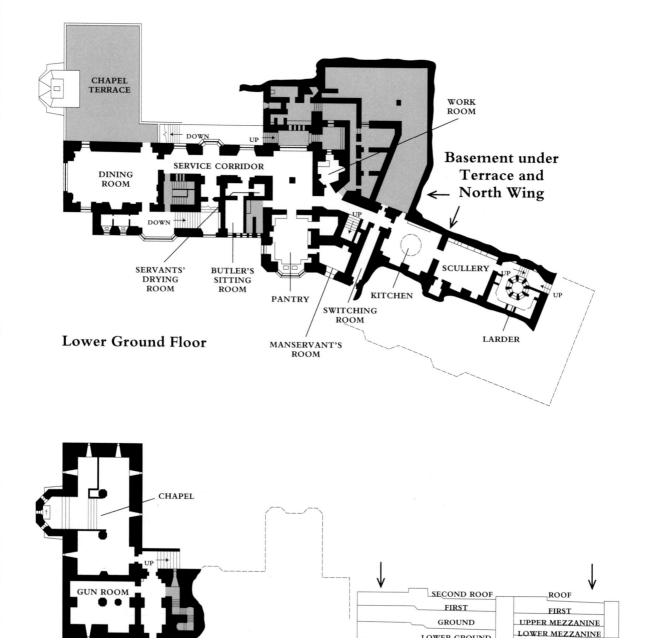

CHAPEL
TERRACE

DOWN   UP

WORK
ROOM

**Basement under
Terrace and
North Wing**

DINING
ROOM

SERVICE CORRIDOR

DOWN

SERVANTS'
DRYING
ROOM

BUTLER'S
SITTING
ROOM

PANTRY

UP

SWITCHING
ROOM

KITCHEN

SCULLERY

UP

UP

LARDER

MANSERVANT'S
ROOM

Lower Ground Floor

CHAPEL

UP

GUN ROOM

SECOND ROOF
FIRST
GROUND
LOWER GROUND
BASEMENT

ROOF
FIRST
UPPER MEZZANINE
LOWER MEZZANINE

Basement under South End

Shaded areas not open to visitors

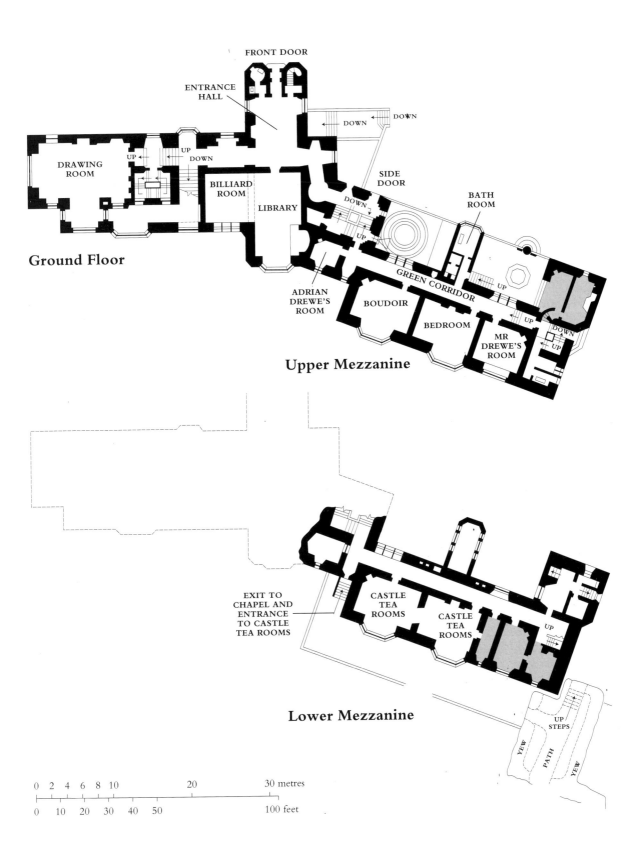

FRONT DOOR

ENTRANCE
HALL

DRAWING
ROOM

UP   UP

DOWN

BILLIARD
ROOM

LIBRARY

Ground Floor

DOWN   DOWN

SIDE
DOOR

BATH
ROOM

DOWN

UP

GREEN CORRIDOR

UP

ADRIAN
DREWE'S
ROOM

BOUDOIR

BEDROOM

MR
DREWE'S
ROOM

UP

DOWN

UP

Upper Mezzanine

EXIT TO
CHAPEL AND
ENTRANCE
TO CASTLE
TEA ROOMS

CASTLE
TEA
ROOMS

CASTLE
TEA
ROOMS

UP

Lower Mezzanine

UP
STEPS

YEW   PATH   YEW

0 2 4 6 8 10   20   30 metres

0 10 20 30 40 50   100 feet

CHAPTER TWO

TOUR OF THE HOUSE

THE ENTRANCE HALL

First reactions on entering the Entrance Hall tend to be conflicting. On the one hand the exotic furnishings of very mixed origin – Spanish, French and English – rub shoulders with surprising ease. On the other the impression of spartan castle life is underlined by bare granite walls and unpainted woodwork, tempered only by the high quality of workmanship and design, whether in the detail of the lion on the iron door-latch, the crisply carved stone or the massive oak doors.

The door panelling is freely adapted from the Perpendicular Gothic and made by Dart & Francis, a Crediton firm which was responsible for most of the castle joinery. Both front doors and two smaller doors on either side, leading to cloakrooms, were fitted in August 1924 at a cost of £263.

FURNITURE

Most of the furnishings are Spanish, reflecting the taste of Adrian de Murietta, a Spanish banker from whom Julius Drewe acquired Wadhurst Hall, in Sussex, in 1899. Some are copies from earlier models: for example, the four cross-framed arm-

The Entrance Hall and Corridor

The Library

chairs were made in the late nineteenth century in a sixteenth-century style. The two coffers are earlier, probably dating from the first half of the eighteenth century, as is the multiple-drawer *vargueño* (drop-front desk) on a stand to the left.

ENAMELS

The four enamel roundels on copper are French, signed 'I.M.'. They come from a set depicting the Seven Planets and are probably by Jean Miette, who is recorded working at Limoges in the 1560s.

THE LIBRARY AND BILLIARD ROOM

This L-shaped room is united by the largest of the arched spans in the castle, built with the aid of a crane. Writing to Julius Drewe in January 1915, John Walker, his agent, reported with relief that it

was finished: 'With an arch of this size one is always anxious that the key is in. There are 49 stones in it, the weight being over 30 tons.' Equally massive are the oak beams it supports, fixed by Dart & Francis five years later, and the vast fireplace, never very practical because it always smokes unless the door is kept open. Nevertheless, this was a popular room with the family, who took tea here on the circular table at the far end, 'a wonderful meal with wafer thin bread and butter, scones and jam and Devonshire cream – and cakes in great variety followed by whatever fruit was in season'. Teatime at Castle Drogo could last for up to two hours.

LIBRARY FURNITURE

The oak bookcases, designed by Lutyens, were almost the last fittings built for the castle, not being in place until March 1931. They contain the residue of Drewe's library, including several runs of local history transactions and a collection of *The Gentle-*

man's Magazine. There are also fourteen volumes of the Rev. George Drew's theological works.

The bulk of the furnishings are English, dating from the nineteenth century; they suggest a comfortable sitting-room, especially the loose-covered armchairs. The roll-top desk in the window is also nineteenth-century but Dutch, and the table football game is probably German, made about 1900. Like most rooms in the castle, the Library had a wireless, which was regarded as 'the height of opulence'. The boudoir grand piano by Challen belonged to Geoffrey Lemmens, a great-grandson of Julius Drewe

TAPESTRIES

It appears from Lutyens's drawings that the Library and Billiard Room were designed to accommodate tapestries from Wadhurst. One from the set of five depicting the Trojan War hangs here, probably made in Brussels in the early seventeenth century. It shows Aeneas carrying his father Anchises from Troy and was bought for Castle Drogo with the aid of the Victoria & Albert Museum and the Royal Oak Foundation.

CERAMICS AND LACQUER

The lustre dishes above the bookcases are Hispano-Moresque and date from the 1700s. The pair of large polychrome Chinese lacquer screens is perhaps mid-eighteenth-century.

METALWORK

The two iron bowls are copies of silver bowls found with the Hildesheim Roman treasure, which was excavated in 1868. The originals are now in Berlin. One portrays the infant Hercules, the other the Greek goddess Athene.

BILLIARD ROOM FURNITURE

Billiard rooms were as much a part of an Edwardian house as a kitchen, and here, with all the trappings, is a full-sized billiard table built by Burroughs & Watts to Lutyens's design. Surrounding it are upholstered leather chairs, which are probably Edwardian but masquerading in seventeenth-century Flemish style. There is also a small oak chest with massive brass hinges inscribed 'Made for Julius C. Drewe by his son Cedric, April 1906'.

(Right)
The Corridor

(Left) Detail from one of the early seventeenth-century tapestries in the Billiard Room

TAPESTRIES

Above the chairs are a second tapestry from the Trojan War set, showing the wooden horse, and an enormous late sixteenth-century Flemish tapestry depicting the story of Judith and Holofernes.

THE CORRIDOR

This provides a link between the Entrance Hall, the Main Stairs and the Drawing Room, involving changes in both level and direction. Lutyens ingeniously combined a tunnel vault with a shallow dome and pendentives to mark the junction with the Staircase and another dome outside the Drawing Room between two short flights of stairs. Originally, the space occupied by the Drawing Room was to have been the upper part of the Dining Room, but in reducing the castle's size the one was built above the other and the stairs added.

PICTURES

ON RIGHT-HAND WALL:

ENGLISH, nineteenth-century
Mary Peek (1821–96)
Julius Drewe's mother, she married the Rev. George Drew in 1845. Her father was a London tea merchant but the Peek family came from Devon, where they can be traced back to the sixteenth century.

ENGLISH, twentieth-century
Adrian Drewe (1891–1917)
Julius Drewe's eldest son, who was killed fighting in Flanders.

ON LEFT-HAND WALL:

CAREL WEIGHT, RA (1908–1998)
Basil Drewe (1894–1974)
Shown seated in front of the Entrance Hall fireplace.

TAPESTRY

This was intended as a *portière* (door curtain). It depicts a florid *Char de Triomphe* (triumphal chariot) designed by Charles Le Brun in 1662 and woven by the Gobelin factory, of which Le Brun was made director the following year.

FURNITURE

The writing-desk in the first window bay is a most unusual Spanish piece dated about 1600. The inlay of bone on walnut depicts the eleven ages of man.

The vast eight-day chiming longcase clock built of mahogany by J. Smith & Sons of Clerkenwell was exhibited at the Paris Exhibition of 1900.

At the top of the stairs are two dummy board figures, probably Spanish, made up from provincial portraits *c*.1600. The pair of stools were used at the 1953 coronation.

THE DRAWING ROOM

It is no accident that the walls of the Drawing Room, traditionally a room for the ladies, were deal-panelled and stipple-painted in green, a colour and technique often used at this time. The room is flooded with light from windows on three sides, which also permit panoramic views of Dartmoor to the south and west and the Teign valley to the east.

On the further side of the valley the stone wall of a Tudor deer-park built for Sir John Whiddon emerges from the bracken-covered slope and Sir John's house can be seen in the middle distance to the south.

The room was used for entertaining and coffee would be served here after dinner.

PICTURES

OVER FIREPLACE:

LOUISA STARR, Mme CANZIANI (1845–1909)
Frances Richardson, Mrs Julius Drewe (1871–1954)
Signed and dated 1909
Frances Richardson married Julius Drewe in 1890.

RIGHT OF FIREPLACE:

LOUISA STARR, Mme CANZIANI (1845–1909)
Adrian Drewe (1891–1917)
Signed
Frances Drewe's eldest son, dressed in a velvet suit like Little Lord Fauntleroy. (The suit and bugle can be seen in the Service Corridor display.)

FURNITURE

Among the chintz-covered sofas (originally upholstered in silk) there are several rarer pieces of furniture. Especially striking are the two bone and mother-of-pearl inlaid tables made in the mid-eighteenth century by German gunmakers. Of the same date, but English, is the pair of gilt gesso mirrors on the end wall. Also English is the handsome set of mahogany chairs in the Chinese Chippendale style, now much restored.

The ebonised tables and cabinets on the fireplace wall come from a variety of sources, the etched ivory pieces to the right of the fireplace being Neapolitan, *c*.1600. The chandeliers are Venetian. Finally, beneath the tapestry, is a Bechstein grand piano in a straight-grained mahogany case which can be exactly dated to 1909.

TAPESTRY

The tapestry on the north wall was probably woven in Brussels in the early eighteenth century. It portrays an episode in the life of Don Quixote after a painting by Teniers.

The Drawing Room

THE MAIN STAIRS

The route from an Edwardian drawing-room to the dining-room was traditionally negotiated with formal ceremony before dinner parties, and at Castle Drogo the Main Stairs offer a marvellous opportunity for processing. They descend in stately fashion around an angle of 90 degrees, within which a secondary staircase runs through the entire four floors. Above them the ceiling is treated in a way that amply illustrates Lutyens's dexterity. It begins as a coffered granite vault until the turn, where another shallow dome eases the change of direction. A further vault between two arches follows, finally developing into an oak-beamed ceiling, but still at the same height as the dome. The distance to the floor is by then 27 feet, allowing an east window of prodigious size. It is made up of 48 lights, with transoms subtly graded to create different propor-

tions in each of the six stages. The Drawing Room is able to borrow light from it through two smaller windows to its right.

PICTURES

AT TOP OF STAIRS:

CHARLES HARDIE, RSA (1858–1916)
Julius Drewe (1856–1931)
Signed and dated 1902
Drewe wears his favourite Burberry and is equipped for fishing on the banks of the Tummel in Perthshire. He holds a book of fishing flies (other examples can be seen in Mr Drewe's Room), and behind him lies a 39lb salmon, which he caught in 1900. The painting lacks vitality and has been criticised for an over-liberal use of brown paint. Lutyens commented about Hardie, 'At least he could paint boots.' The salmon has been preserved;

15

mounted and cased, it can be seen in one of the two rooms used as a restaurant in the castle.

FACING AT FOOT OF STAIRS:

CHARLES HARDIE, RSA (1858–1916)
Frances Richardson, Mrs Julius Drewe (1871–1954)
Signed and dated 1902
A companion piece to the above, and a more successful painting. She is shown standing in the rose garden at Wadhurst. Her daughter once described her as 'a tall, slender and very graceful figure with fair hair and blue eyes, and I always remember her beautiful white dresses and sunshades and lovely jewellery, presents from my father, especially her rings – a very beautiful and attractive person – and she and my father were constant companions...'.

TO LEFT:

BINNY MATHEWS (b.1960)
Anthony Drewe, MC (1920–91)
Signed and dated 1989
The eldest grandson of Julius and Frances Drewe, he and his son Christopher gave Castle Drogo to the National Trust in 1974. He is shown in front of a Spanish leather screen in the family's private drawing-room at Drogo. Commissioned by the Trust's Foundation for Art.

THE DINING ROOM

After the grandeur of the staircase, the Dining Room is an anticlimax, the result of a compromise reached in 1912 when the castle's size was drastically reduced. Before that date the room was planned to rise through two storeys with the great hall and drawing-room to its west. After 1912 the great hall was dispensed with and the upper half of the Dining Room sacrificed for the Drawing Room. The result is a long low room, an impression reinforced by the heavily decorated plaster ceiling installed by Crockers of Plymouth. The walls are panelled in Cuban mahogany and Lutyens's inventiveness makes its mark once again in the plain granite frieze between the carved Corinthian order pilasters. The panelling and that in the Drawing Room is by the Rugby firm J. Parnell and Son.

The room was first used over Christmas in 1928 and thereafter all meals except tea were served here;

(Left)
The Dining Room

(Right)
The Main Stairs

A Battle Scene: The Turks and Austrians fighting before Vienna in 1683 (Dining Room)

dinner, generally at 7.30pm, was the occasion when family and guests, the men in dinner jackets, would meet summoned by a gong. Grace would be said and a menu, in French, studied for a choice of three courses served by the butler and under-butler. Children ate separately in the upstairs nursery. Lutyens himself was occasionally a guest and once amused his host by using the mustard and wine to draw pictures on his menu card.

Mr and Mrs Drewe were slow eaters and meals could last for up to two hours. Their daughter, Frances, described how the table was laid:

They always had a damask cloth, never mats – and my Father was very proud of an electric cloth which was put under the damask cloth and they put candlesticks at the four corners which pricked in with little connections into the electric cloth for lighting the table candles. My Mother was rather fond of Worcester china and there were rather elaborate china figures in the middle of the table and at the four corners with ferns growing in them. Then at night rather heavy elaborate floral arrangements in cut glass and silver table centres sometimes with the light under them, done by the gardener or footman.

PICTURES

CLOCKWISE, FROM ENTRANCE DOOR:

J. EMERY
William Peek (1791–1870)
Signed and dated 1851
He founded the tea firm William Peek & Co. *c.* 1810. His daughter Mary (below) married the Rev. George Smith Drew. Julius Drewe was their son.

OVER FIREPLACE:

LOUISA STARR, Mme CANZIANI (1845–1909)
Mary Peek, Mrs George Drew (1821–96)
Signed and dated 1898
Mother of Julius Drewe.

ENGLISH, nineteenth-century
Mary Francis, Mrs William Peek (1804–74)
Wife and mother of the above.

ENGLISH, nineteenth-century
On either side of the *Battle Scene* is a portrait of an anonymous Peek relation.

ANONYMOUS
A Battle Scene: The Turks and Austrians fighting before Vienna in 1683
Bears signature and date *Lucas Kranacht 1597*
In 1683 the Ottoman army was routed by a largely Polish force commanded by King John Sobieski III. The red and white national colours and the eagle of Poland can be seen on the banners, and the winged armour is characteristic of the Polish hussars. The picture was apparently bought by Julius Drewe for Kilmorie, his Torquay home, from Sir Thomas Bailey.

END WALL:

GILBERT BOWLEY
The Rev. George Smith Drew (1819–80)
Signed
Father of Julius Drewe.

GEORGE HARCOURT, RA (1868–1947)
Julius Drewe (1856–1931)
Signed and dated 1931
Seated in front of one of the castle's tapestries depicting scenes from the Old Testament. His appearance is recognisable from a description written by his daughter:

He always wore a light fancy waistcoat and never the one belonging to his suit and my Mother always said there were any amount of waistcoats in the drawer belonging to his suits that were never used. He wore this light waistcoat with his gold watch and chain and he always wore a finely knitted tie of an off-white shade and a diamond tie pin, and a silver top walking stick.

ENGLISH, nineteenth-century
George Drewe (1790–1867)
Grandfather of Julius Drewe.

FURNISHINGS

The dining-table is still laid with a damask cloth, the electric candlesticks and Worcester china, and sets of Venetian glass bought by Mr and Mrs Drewe on their honeymoon. The stamped leather chairs reflect de Murietta's Spanish taste, but the smaller dining-chairs are English, dating from the end of the

nineteenth century. A heavily restored table against the wall supports a pair of silver-plate mounted horns from Scandinavia. The copper warming-plates, behind the leather screen, were a useful accessory, as the Kitchen is 50 yards away down the Service Corridor. They were regularly used for breakfast at 8.45am every morning when a choice of bacon, eggs, sausages and fish was normal.

In the corridor immediately outside is a napkin press, to ensure that crisp linen was always available.

THE SERVICE CORRIDOR

The corridor leads to 'below stairs', an area seldom penetrated by the family, but nevertheless as carefully designed by Lutyens as the rest of the house: the ceiling is alternately arched and vaulted, and the granite immaculately finished. Half-way to the Kitchen the corridor meets the junction where the main block of the house joins the north wing, and an octagonal granite column marks the approximate centre of the castle. Routes from here link the Kitchen, the Pantry and the boiler room.

PICTURE

CHARLES HARDIE, RSA (1858–1916)
Mary Drewe (1900–85)
Signed and dated 1902
Mary is depicted in the garden at Wadhurst clutching a favourite soft toy (shown in the case opposite).

TOYS

Children's toys now fill the window and wall embrasures, including a fine doll's-house made for the Drewes' elder daughter Mary in 1906 by William Hodder, the estate carpenter at Wadhurst.

On the right-hand side is a detailed lobby furnished with a glazed niche containing Adrian Drewe's velvet suit, see in the portrait above.

THE BUTLER'S SITTING ROOM

Mr and Mrs Rayner, butler and cook respectively, created this sitting room out of a store. Their bedroom was in the north tower. The room never had a fireplace but Mrs Rayner had a mantelpiece installed so she could display her favourite clock.

The Rayners left the castle in the late 1930s but Mrs Rayner returned as cook in 1944.

THE SERVANTS' DRYING ROOM

Resident staff did their washing in the nearby washroom and dried the clothes here. The pipes running under the slatted floor are original and were heated by the castle's hot water system.

Visitors should continue along the Service Corridor.

LUTYENS COLLECTION

At the junction is a varied collection of items relating to Lutyens himself. The three large perspective drawings of the castle are worth comparing; the central one shows the south front at its most ambitious stage in 1911 and on either side are careful studies by Cyril Farey of the castle, virtually as built in 1924. These two were bought with the help of the National Art Collections Fund. The architectural

models of other Lutyens houses were made especially for the 1981 Lutyens Exhibition in London and donated to the National Trust by the Arts Council.

Two of Lutyens's personal possessions, an Indian painting acquired while working at Delhi, and a cabinet of his own design, are also here, kindly loaned by the architect's grandson.

The architect's chair, probably designed by Lutyens, was made for the architectural historian Nathaniel Lloyd who lived at Great Dixter.

THE PANTRY

This room has barely changed since it was last in daily use in 1954. The oak cupboards, still filled with china, the table and the teak sinks were all designed by Lutyens and made by Dart & Francis in 1927. In one corner is the usual country house bell board and a telephone exchange. The first telephone link was established in 1915 and from here external calls could be directed to and from the eighteen telephones within the house.

Two doors lead from the Pantry, one to the manservant's bed-sitting-room, strategically placed next to the other, a large walk-in safe where the silver was kept. The Heals furniture in the former was made in 1927.

THE WORK ROOM

The room was designed as a servant's bedroom but soon became a work room and store. The fittings and contents are all indigenous.

THE SWITCHROOM

Visitors next pass the staircase to the ground floor, the wicker door of the lift, incorporated in the building from its inception, and the open door of the still operative Switchroom. This houses terminals for electricity brought direct to the castle from two turbines harnessed to the River Teign as well as the more conventional alternating current supply and the power supply for the lift. Those who knew Castle Drogo before the war recall that it was heated by 'hundreds of electric fires' plugged into any of

The Switchroom

332 sockets. Another electric gadget, popular in the 1930s, was a centralised vacuum-cleaning system built under the floorboards of the rooms.

At a lower level, beneath the castle forecourt, is a boiler room (not open to visitors), which powers the hot water and radiator heating systems. In a rather petulant letter to John Walker in February 1929, Julius Drewe complained:

The heat given off at present by the radiators outside the dining room is not one tenth of what is necessary and rather than not have enough heat now provided I would like to have double the quantity that is considered absolutely necessary.

THE KITCHEN

In the 1930s this was presided over by the cook, London-trained Mrs Rayner, whose standard of cuisine 'was very high'. The two coal ranges she

cooked on were removed in 1945, but replaced with a similar pair by the National Trust. The originals, marketed as 'the Kooksjoie', were always immaculately blackleaded. All the other furniture was designed by Lutyens and remains intact – notably the circular beechwood table. Its shape echoes the circular lantern above, which provides the only natural light in the room. Mrs Drewe thought this insufficient and suggested that 'a glint of sun' should somehow be contrived. Lutyens disagreed, unwilling no doubt to upset the symmetry of his design. Distemper, he argued, was enough, and as so often, his views prevailed.

THE SCULLERY

The room, serviced by a scullery maid and kitchen maids, had two functions: washing up in the three sinks beneath the long rows of plate racks, and food

The Kitchen

The Scullery

preparation. Against the two granite monolithic columns Lutyens placed a hexagonal chopping-block, now deeply scarred, and an enormous pestle and mortar. Quenelles were one of Mrs Rayner's specialities and the rumbling from the huge pestle and mortar she used to prepare them could be heard throughout much of the castle. Another range once filled the recess where a wood-burning stove stands today. To its right is the lift which transported food to the servants' hall on the floor above and the nurseries two floors beyond that. Again, the room is top-lit, but this time by lunettes above sills joggled into position.

THE LARDER

Lutyens ingeniously fulfilled the practical require-

ments of a larder by building it around an octagonal well, below ground level. In this way plenty of fresh air and shady subdued light were achieved. Traditional slate shelves and granite walls add to the coolness. A short flight of steps leads to the back door, where produce from the garden could be delivered into a specially designed vegetable rack with sliding doors. Beyond this door (accessible from outside) were the ash-house and washroom, now converted into lavatories.

THE NORTH TOWER STAIRCASE

The North Tower was used as a service wing and in creating this separate staircase, Lutyens ensured that the paths of servants and family would not cross unnecessarily. This was usual in large country houses, and a member of the family recalling a stay at the castle in the 1920s illustrates the effect:

There must have been a staff comparable in size to that at Wadhurst, but we seldom saw many of the servants. The cleaning and dusting downstairs would be done by the housemaids before the family came down to breakfast, and our bedrooms would always be 'done' when we were out. Our clothes, often left littered about the room, would be carefully put away, our suits pressed, shoes cleaned, riding breeches scrubbed and pressed and our evening clothes put out ready on the bed. As at Wadhurst, there was a separate laundry which dealt with all the washing and ironing.

Such a clear distinction between above and below stairs did not, however, extend to the building itself, for there is no lack of quality in the granite used in the North Tower nor in the staircase that climbs through its five floors. This staircase is especially remarkable for the oak balustrade which stands independently of the cantilevered granite steps, another example of Lutyens's inventiveness.

The rent table in Mr Drewe's Room

THE GREEN CORRIDOR

Running the length of the north wing, this corridor is the middle one of three similar corridors. That above serves the nursery (now a flat, and not open to the public) and that below the staff quarters (now the restaurant and Kitchen). This corridor links a suite of rooms which were the first in the castle to be inhabited by Mr and Mrs Drewe. On the outside wall the deep window embrasures are divided by slender granite slabs, six feet high, but only three inches thick, a tribute to the masons' skill.

PICTURES

The walls were once hung with tapestries, but now have pictures: watercolours by Mrs Frances Richardson, Julius Drewe's mother-in-law, and lithographs of Dartmoor. The sheepdog in the portrait, named 'Trusty', was the pet of the Drewes' younger daughter Frances.

TEXTILES AND FURNITURE

The green carpet, like others in the bedrooms, is a recent copy of one which was made specially for the

house in 1928. At the far end of the corridor is a Spanish cupboard, another piece from Wadhurst.

MR DREWE'S ROOM ·

This oak-panelled room was used by Julius Drewe during the short time he lived at Castle Drogo before his death in 1931. It is comfortably cluttered, reflecting several of his interests, chief among them being his family, portrayed in the portrait photographs, and the business world, symbolised by the company seal on the rent table. The table was originally downstairs in what is now the restaurant and is a substitute for the bed which used to be here. The case of fishing flies, the cigar cabinet (in which he packed his cigars in green tea to keep them fresh), and gadgets like the electric cup warmer are all the characteristic paraphernalia of an Edwardian gentleman.

PICTURES

The two large portraits of Mrs George Drew and Mrs Thomas Richardson, mothers of Julius Drewe and his wife Frances respectively, are opaltypes (photographs printed on ground opal glass) and of exceptional quality.

23

The Bathroom

FURNITURE

Furnishings were brought from Wadhurst, and are a *mélange* of eighteenth-century English pieces, such as the revolving rent table, and more up-to-date pieces typical of an Edwardian household, such as the Benares table, a large gentleman's wardrobe and the cross-framed chair near the table. This chair, Tudor in style, bears the label of a Tottenham Court Road furniture store.

THE BATHROOM

Opposite, the Bathroom is contained within its own small wing (the nursery pantry is sited on the floor above), which projects at right angles from the main building to meet the curtain wall around the Kitchen quarters below.

An idiosyncratic Lutyens feature is the dais at the far end of the room, serving simply as a convenient place to sit. The bath itself is a developed version of a model first produced in the late nineteenth century which includes a complex shower unit at its business end. It was restored to working order in 1992. In all, seven baths were supplied to the castle after Julius Drewe had personally chosen the design from Messrs Boulding in London.

The WC, off the corridor, supplied by the same firm, is similar to several others in the castle, fitted with a mahogany seat and side-pull, siphonic flush.

THE BEDROOM

The room is furnished to resemble its appearance when used as a bedroom by Mr and Mrs Julius Drewe. Most of the contents were brought from Wadhurst, and it demonstrates the Edwardians' interest in late eighteenth-century furniture, usually French-inspired, and their lack of scruples about introducing reproduction pieces where originals were unavailable. It is also a room where family photographs are on display, as the Drewes were devoted parents and grandparents.

Superb views of the Teign Gorge can be seen from the window. In the early morning sunlight deer are sometimes spotted browsing in the bracken and gorse which grows almost up to the castle's walls.

THE BOUDOIR

Like the other rooms on this corridor, the Boudoir is oak-panelled and modest in size. It was Mrs Drewe's sitting-room and is agreeably furnished with comfortable eighteenth-century-style tables and chairs, carpet-upholstered armchairs and a Bechstein piano. In the glass-fronted fitted cupboards is a wonderful mixture of souvenirs, curiosities and favourite books.

Traditionally, the room has been hung with pictures and still is, but with oil paintings now loaned from elsewhere.

ADRIAN DREWE'S ROOM

Adrian was Julius Drewe's eldest son, born in 1891. He was educated at Eton and Cambridge before studying medicine at Bart's. With the outbreak of the First World War he joined the Royal Garrison Artillery and attained the rank of Major. He married in 1916, but on 12 July 1917 was killed in action at Ypres, leaving no children. He had been involved in the planning of Castle Drogo from the start and Mr and Mrs Drewe were deeply affected by his death. A bedroom at Wadhurst was converted into a Memorial Room in his honour and in due course this was re-established at Castle Drogo.

Adrian Drewe, the Drewes' eldest son, who was killed at the Battle of Ypres in 1917; a hand-coloured 'crayon' photograph (Adrian Drewe's Room)

The Chapel

School and college mementoes line the walls and fill the cabinet.

PICTURES AND SCULPTURE

The large full-length portrait is a hand-coloured gelatine bromide 'crayon' photograph of Adrian Drewe in uniform. Beneath it is a bronze figure of Victory commissioned by Julius Drewe in memory of his son. It is unsigned but the base is engraved

with battle honours. Adrian had been mentioned in despatches before his death at the age of 26.

THE CASTLE TEA ROOMS

Apart from the Drawing Room, this is the only room in the house where the panelling was painted, in this case a matt white to lighten the interior, now hung with etchings depicting scenes from the Franco-Prussian War.

The room was originally designed as the Servants' Hall, in other words a sitting-room for domestic staff and the venue for the annual servants' ball. The number of living-in servants varied but there was generally a nucleus of butler, under-butler, cook, scullery and kitchen maids, head housemaid, under-housemaid, two ladies' maids, nanny and nursery maid. Although the family enjoyed a privileged existence, it was also true that the servants were well looked after. Private medical care was always available to them and on retirement a pension would be paid.

The adjoining restaurant room is fitted out with cupboards in each corner and was formerly used as an office. The three oars were Adrian Drewe's, used by him when rowing at Cambridge University. The salmon over the chimney-piece is the same one shown in the portrait of Julius Drewe at the top of the Main Stairs.

Visitors should turn right at the bottom of the stairs and leave the castle by the Castle Tea Room door. Once outside turn left along the gravel path. To visit the Chapel and Gun Room, turn right at the end of the path, follow signs across the grass, and they are on your left.

THE GUN ROOM

Like the Chapel, the Gun Room is vaulted and very sturdily built, for above it are the Dining Room, Drawing Room and a bedroom floor. The equipment for the traditional country pursuits of shooting and fishing was kept here and a granite sink provided for cleaning fish caught in the Teign. Both Julius and Basil Drewe fished the river, which yielded salmon weighing up to 20lb, trout and sea trout from the pool below the turbines. Pheasant and partridge were, for a while, reared on the estate.

Today the room is furnished with museum cases containing drawings, letters and photographs which illustrate the castle's construction and other educational information.

THE CHAPEL

Julius Drewe was an old-fashioned evangelical; he taught at the Sunday School each week in the chapel at Wadhurst, so it was natural for him to plan a place of worship at Castle Drogo. Lutyens's earliest drawings show a two-storey apse-ended chapel at the north-west side of the courtyard plan, but with drastic reductions in the size of the castle, a much smaller version was formed within the undercroft beneath the abandoned great hall, where the walls are six feet thick and the windows small.

After so many spacious views and light-filled rooms the descent into this apparently subterranean room creates a surprising contrast. The three-bay interior is groin-vaulted, with granite once again laboriously fashioned for the pair of massive monolithic columns and the chequered blocks along the groins.

FURNISHINGS

The altar rails, lectern, font and stained glass were brought from Wadhurst; the pews, rebuilt by Dart & Francis, were, with the organ, the last fittings to be made for the castle, in 1931. Consecration finally took place in September of that year, only two months before Julius Drewe's death.

The wooden cross against the entrance wall once marked Adrian Drewe's grave in Flanders. Adjacent is a photograph of the permanent headstone which replaced it and details of Adrian's death. In the far aisle is a model of Lutyens's Thiepval Arch (1927–32), the Memorial to the Missing of the British Empire on the Somme. At Lutyens's insistence, it was non-denominational:

All that is done of structure should be for all time and for equality of honours, for besides Christians of all denominations, there will be Jews, Musselmens, Hindus and men of other creeds; their glorious names and their mortal bodies all equally deserving enduring record and seemly sepulture.

Lutyens also designed the Cenotaph in Whitehall and the Great War Stone for the British war cemeteries on the Western Front.

27

THE GARDEN AND OUTBUILDINGS

HISTORY

Lutyens's first plans, drawn in 1915, were for a formal garden on the east side of the house with a central axis path aligned with the bay window of the Library and from there to the front door. Above this path was a tree circle that transformed into an avenue, solving the awkward change of axis at the point where the house itself is hinged. By 1921 this scheme had developed to include a currently fashionable feature, a rill which channelled water from the house into two pools, before descending into a larger pool in the centre of a circular lawn. The entire garden was enclosed within yew hedges. Below it were hanging gardens in the Italian style and a patchwork of herbaceous beds.

Sadly this ambitious plan was eventually rejected because Mr Drewe believed the terracing would obstruct his view of the river and it contained too many steps; besides, 'the servants will have a full view of the gardens'. Instead in 1922 the landscape gardening firm of R. Wallace & Co. of Tunbridge Wells was employed to produce new plans. A partner in the firm, George Dillistone, had previously

The rose garden

advised Julius Drewe on the planting at Wadhurst and it is intriguing to compare that garden with his plans for Castle Drogo.

Straight away the eastern site was rejected and a new one chosen, quite separate from the castle, to the north-west. It is known that at Wadhurst the garden comprised a rose garden, three terraces and a croquet lawn surrounded by yew hedges. Roses were a particular favourite of Mrs Drewe; her portrait in the house shows her on the rose terrace at Wadhurst, so it is no surprise to find roses at Castle Drogo, but Dillistone's influence is also seen in the

(Left) The yew hedges in the rose garden

formal system of terracing and the vast croquet or tennis lawn, once again hedged with yews. In 1920 Dillistone had written a book, *The Planning and Planting of Little Gardens*, in which he emphasised the importance of design: 'The garden is an artificial creation for a specific purpose. It is the room of the house that is out of doors. As man's handiwork it should bear the indelible stamp of man's art and craft.' At Castle Drogo this theory was fulfilled.

At one stage in the 1920s Lutyens planned an avenue approach to the south end of the garden, linked to the house and a crescent-shaped stables and garage block, but this came to nothing. The garage block, when eventually completed was surprisingly modest considering the magnificent vehicles housed within. Apart from traditional carriages, there were

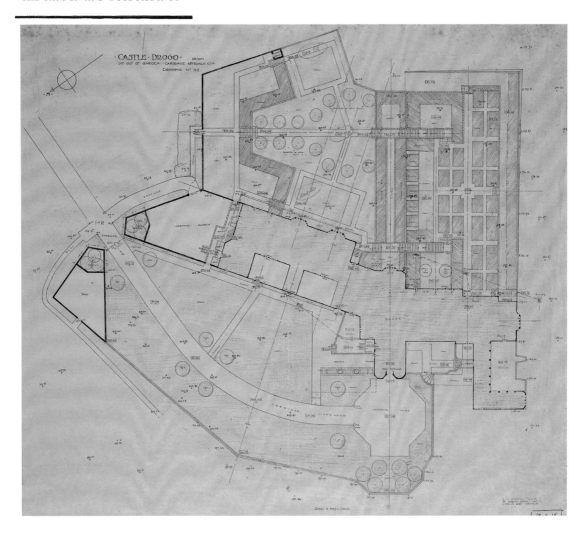

Lutyens's 1915 design for the garden and drive

always cars, first represented by a Clément, followed by a Spycka and finally two Silver Ghost Rolls-Royces. These were driven by the chauffeur and used in alternate years until sold in 1937 for £5 each. (It was typical of Mr Drewe's attention to detail that the size of the forecourt and the gravel was determined only after he had practised turning circles in his car.) In the adjoining stables there were always a Dartmoor pony or two and hunters which were regularly exercised.

To the west of the stables the land drops steeply, and in the 1950s Basil Drewe and his wife had the inspired idea of planting it with rhododendrons, tree magnolias, camellias, cherries and maples, allowing the blossom to be observed from above on the terrace walk. Rhododendrons, both species and hybrid, were Basil Drewe's particular passion, which he brought in from his previous garden, from the Royal Horticultural Society and from Wallace's nursery.

The only garden near the castle is at the approach to the Chapel. The small lawned area is overwhelmed by echoing granite walls which shelter a huge fig tree, a camellia and a *Garrya elliptica*, distinguished by its tassel-like flowers during winter and early spring.

The kitchen garden, which was sited in a sheltered valley to the south, well beyond the castle, no longer survives.

Originally, the gardens were cared for by a head gardener and six others. Today there are two gardeners.

TOUR OF THE FORMAL GARDEN

A series of yew hedges link the castle to the garden, the latter protected by a wind break of mainly Beech and Scot's Pine. At 1,000 ft this is the National Trust's highest garden which also endures fierce winds and an annual rainfall of 45 inches per year. The formal garden is divided into three terraces. The lowest has at its centre 24 flower beds containing a mixture of modern and old English roses and modern Hybrid Tea and Floribunda roses. The two flanking borders are planted with predominantly white flowers such as *Aster, Viminalis, Hydrangea quercifolia* and *Galtonaia candicans*. Beneath the almost round-stoned granite retaining walls are a selection of spring flowering plants including, *Euphorbia wulfenii, Daphne collina* and *Narcissus "Barrett Browning"*. At the corners of this terrace are formal groups of trees each forming a shady arbour. Originally the trees were weeping elms but these succumbed to Dutch elm disease and were replaced in 1981 by Persian Ironwood trees, *Parrotia Persica*. The herbaceous borders either side of the terrace are divided by distinctive twisting paths whose design was borrowed by Lutyens from a pattern he had seen in India. The planting is inspired by Dillistone's original scheme using colour, texture, height and scent continuously throughout the year. Plants include *Geranium endressii, Aconitum napellus, Echinops ritro, Iris germanica* and *Leucanthemum × superbum*. The plants are supported using birch "pea sticks" from the gorge and identified by traditional labels.

At the head of the steps to the second terrace are original groups of *Yucca recurvifolia* and *Wisteria sinensis*. The base of the Wisteria wall is planted with *Abelia × grandiflora, Crinum × powellii* and a pomegranate (*Punica Granatum*) from a pip planted by one of the Drewe family. The herb borders were replanted in the spring of 1989 in order to recreate

The Bunty House

what Dillistone described in a letter to Basil Drewe in September 1929 as a "fragrant garden". This gives scope to use plants such as chives (*Allium schoenoprasum*), Sweet Bay (*Laurus nobilis*) and Chocolate Cosmos (*Cosmus atrosanguinea*).

A double flight of steps leads up to the shrub borders designed by Dillistone in 1927. For these borders he chose many of his favourite plants including *Acer palmatum, Cotinus coggyria* and *Hamamelis mollis* (Witch Hazel). The azaleas that flank the path provide spring colour whilst *Lilium lancifolium* (Tiger Lily) repeat the theme in late summer.

The axial path continues to lead on and up to the anticipated climax in this most architectural of gardens. A pair of Cyprus trees flanks an opening in the yew hedge but on passing through one is confronted by a circular lawn surrounded by the hedge and nothing else. However, it is so vast and such a surprise that there is no sense of anticlimax, quite the opposite. It has always had an entirely practical purpose, being used for tennis and croquet.

North of the entrance to the circular lawn is a little cottage garden attached to the Bunty House, a children's playroom modelled on a 1930s suburban house which Julius Drewe bought for his grandchildren. It has its own little woodland garden with spring flowering bulbs such as *Camassia leichtlinii caerulea, Fritillaria meleagris* and *Crocus tommasinianus*.

CHAPTER FOUR
THE ESTATE

Traditionally, the English country house has been supported from income generated by the surrounding estate. However, Julius Drewe had made his money in trade, so when he decided to set himself up as a country gentleman, he could afford to enjoy the acres he had bought simply as a dramatic view (the land had always been of marginal value agriculturally).

The Castle Drogo estate lies in and above the valley of the River Teign, with land on both sides of the river as it leaves the Chagford basin, and enters a deep gorge section below the castle itself.

The two prominent tors which rise above the gorge dramatically show the change in rock type which splits the estate nearly in two. To the west Hunter's Tor, with its rounded granite boulders, marks the edge of the area underlain by Dartmoor granite, while to the east is Sharp Tor, made of carboniferous Culm Measures (slates, mudstones, siltstones) thermally metamorphosed by the adjacent granite. The result is a range of habitats, particularly broad-leaved woodland, dwarf-shrub heathland, riverine communities, farmland and the ancient Whiddon deer-park.

The last is perhaps the most important area of the estate and is an outstanding example of an old medieval deer-park, surrounded by an impressive granite stone wall some eight feet high. It contains fine old trees, mostly oak and ash, which support an extremely rich lichen flora (of European importance). Lichens require clean air and, more significantly, the high numbers of different lichen species present signify an unchanged history of management. Some species are extremely old. The continuity of management and resulting mature timber has also meant that the park is rich in 'old forest' invertebrates – that is, species whose survival has depended on there being long continuity of mature and over-mature (dead wood) timber. The

park has been declared a Site of Special Scientific Interest and consequently the National Trust promotes far less access than to most other parts of the estate.

Adjoining the park and cladding the south side of the gorge opposite Sharp Tor, Whiddon Wood reflects man's activities from a later period. Almost totally made up of oak, these woods are intensively worked as coppice woodland.

Coppicing is a rotational system of cropping timber, no longer practised commercially in Devon. Some species of tree have the ability to re-grow multiple stems after being cut to ground level. Hazel, oak, sweet chestnut and ash were extensively cut using this system each year, moving on to another section of the wood the following year. With oak the rotation was about 25 years. Oak bark has a high tannin content, so after cutting it was peeled off the wood in strips and taken for use in the leather-curing industry. The remaining timber was burnt slowly in earth-covered mounds to produce charcoal. Many of these charcoal-burning sites can still be seen as small platforms dotted here and there throughout the woods. The oak woods are also home to fallow deer thought to have escaped from the deer-park, and to birds such as the pied flycatcher and woodwarbler, both summer migrants.

On the castle side of the gorge is a completely different habitat – open heathland. Yet here too it is man's activity that has shaped the landscape. The slopes of the gorge were once covered with trees but were cleared to provide rough grazing in the form of common land. Piddledown Common, as it is known, once extended right across the agricultural fields above the gorge, but now the level land is

(Right) The view south-east from the roof towards Dartmoor

improved with fertilisers and modern grass-seed mixes, leaving only the steep slopes as a remnant of how it once appeared. The combination of poor soils and a history of grazing over the centuries has produced a classic dwarf heathland. Bell heather (*Erica cinerea*) and western gorse (*Ulex gallii*) dominate, producing spectacular colours in the summer.

The rocky tors support an open lichen heath of good quality with substantial populations of the nationally scarce toadflax-leaved St John's wort (*Hypericum linarifolium*) and a species of ant, *Leptothorax tuberum*, which in Britain is almost totally confined to cliffs on the south coast, making this inland site exceptional.

Many of the 25 species of butterfly found on the estate frequent the heathland – green hairstreak, grayling, pearl-bordered and small pearl-bordered fritillaries are common, and if you are very lucky the nationally rare high brown fritillary can be seen among the bracken-covered fringes.

After the Second World War marginal land like the gorge area became uneconomic, and grazing ceased, so that it reverted to woodland. Photographs taken at the time the castle was built show clearly that there were no trees on the heathland. Today we can see how invasive tree species such as birch are slowly spreading, smothering the very special heathland flora and fauna.

By managing the countryside it is possible to achieve a balance of every type of habitat, and to this end the National Trust aims to remove most of the recent invasive trees in the gorge. In order to maintain open heathland in future years, ponies have been reintroduced to browse unwanted tree seedlings and break up the dense stands of gorse. Small, controlled burns will also take place, aimed particularly at producing a healthy new growth of heather. All this work will take place in the autumn and winter months so as not to disturb wildlife, especially nesting birds such as stonechat, tree and meadow pipits.

The River Teign and its environment should not be forgotten either. Over thousands of years the river cut its powerful way down through the rocks to form the gorge, changing from a placid idyllic stream in summer to a raging torrent after heavy rain on the moors.

Not far downstream of the weir on the north side of the river is the logan stone, a massive block of granite balanced on top of another on the river bank. The stone seems once to have moved to and fro, and was a popular tourist site. John Swete describes it in his diary for 1792:

We reached the 'Moving Rock', a stupendous block of granite, detached and resting on its base on a rising narrow point of another mass, deep grounded in the channel of the river an equipoise was thus wonderfully formed . . . the dimensions of this stone are enormous! At the west point it is ten feet high and from west to east the length is about eighteen feet [an exaggeration].

Dippers and kingfishers are a common sight along the river and in autumn salmon leap up the fish ladder by the weir. Otters have often been seen, but visitor numbers may be too high for them to settle and breed.

The estate is covered by a series of public footpaths, bridleways, National Trust permitted tracks and, in the woods, many timber extraction rides. The Trust encourages access but would ask that visitors respect the code of the countryside by staying on marked paths, shutting all gates when found to be shut, and keeping dogs on a lead when stock are nearby.

The logan stone; engraving by W. and G. Cooke, 1805

FAMILY TREE

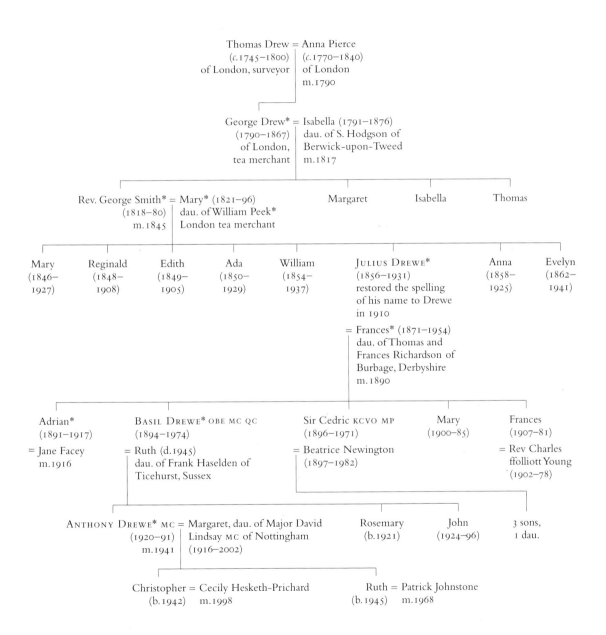

Thomas Drew = Anna Pierce
(*c*.1745–1800)   (*c*.1770–1840)
of London, surveyor   of London
m.1790

George Drew* = Isabella (1791–1876)
(1790–1867)   dau. of S. Hodgson of
of London,   Berwick-upon-Tweed
tea merchant   m.1817

Rev. George Smith* = Mary* (1821–96)   Margaret   Isabella   Thomas
(1818–80)   dau. of William Peek*
m.1845   London tea merchant

Mary   Reginald   Edith   Ada   William   JULIUS DREWE*   Anna   Evelyn
(1846–   (1848–   (1849–   (1850–   (1854–   (1856–1931)   (1858–   (1862–
1927)   1908)   1905)   1929)   1937)   restored the spelling   1925)   1941)
of his name to Drewe
in 1910

= Frances* (1871–1954)
dau. of Thomas and
Frances Richardson of
Burbage, Derbyshire
m.1890

Adrian*   BASIL DREWE* OBE MC QC   Sir Cedric KCVO MP   Mary   Frances
(1891–1917)   (1894–1974)   (1896–1971)   (1900–85)   (1907–81)

= Jane Facey   = Ruth (d.1945)   = Beatrice Newington   = Rev Charles
m.1916   dau. of Frank Haselden of   (1897–1982)   ffolliott Young
Ticehurst, Sussex   (1902–78)

ANTHONY DREWE* MC = Margaret, dau. of Major David   Rosemary   John   3 sons,
(1920–91)   Lindsay MC of Nottingham   (b.1921)   (1924–96)   1 dau.
m.1941   (1916–2002)

Christopher = Cecily Hesketh-Prichard   Ruth = Patrick Johnstone
(b.1942)   m.1998   (b.1945)   m.1968

Owners of Castle Drogo are shown in CAPITALS   Asterisk denotes portrait in the house

CHAPTER FIVE

THE FAMILY BACKGROUND

Although Castle Drogo is renowned as the largest and one of the last country houses built this century, its history is a traditional tale of Victorian enterprise centred on one man, Julius Drewe, whose career in the retail trade was spectacular by any standards. In 1883 with a loan of £10,000 he and his partner, John Musker, opened a shop in London known as the Home and Colonial Stores. Six years later the business had expanded at such a rate that both were wealthy men and able to retire from active participation in the company. Drewe was only 33 years old, but had all the resources necessary to build a country seat in which to establish his growing family.

Julius Drewe's grandfather, George Drew, who was a London tea merchant (Dining Room)

Julius Drew had been born at Pulloxhill near Ampthill in Bedfordshire in 1856, the sixth child of the local vicar, the Rev. George Smith Drew, a difficult, scholarly character who, it was said, might have become a bishop had he been a more tactful person. Instead, after several incumbencies as parish priest he became Hulsean lecturer at Cambridge three years before his death in 1880.

The Rev. Drew's father had been a tea broker in Marylebone and his wife, Mary Peek, came from a family which also had a long history in the tea trade. It was natural, therefore, that the young Julius should go into the business. He joined the tea importing firm of Peek Bros. & Winch, which had been established in Liverpool by Mrs Drew's brother Francis. Julius became a tea buyer in the Far East where he celebrated his 21st birthday before returning to England and promotion as the firm's representative in Liverpool. After the excitement of travel the job lacked the sort of challenge Julius Drew enjoyed, so in 1878 he opened his own Liverpool shop, 'The Willow Pattern Tea Store'. It was a shrewd move but Drew lacked retailing experience and therefore, in 1883, he took on Musker, who had that expertise, as his partner. Their joint venture was to open the London shop in the Edgware Road.

This was a period of rapid expansion and change in the retail industry, which saw the rise of the multiple store, of advertising and the brand name. John James Sainsbury had opened his first dairy in Drury Lane in 1869, Thomas Lipton his first grocery in Glasgow in 1871. Drew, Sainsbury and Lipton all prospered with the growth of the urban working class, who wanted wholesome basic food at keen prices. Drew expanded the Home and Colonial Stores from its London base, opening big stores in Birmingham and Leeds, which, like the Edgware Road headquarters, stocked a wide range

Julius Drewe; painted by George Harcourt, 1931 (Dining Room)

of lines. These were complemented by smaller specialist shops, which were known as 'tea stores'. By 1890 there were 107 shops all over the country, managed by a new limited company.

Drew himself did all the buying, particularly of Indian tea, thereby causing a minor social revolution, since it was his shops that encouraged the swing in public taste from China to Indian tea. Butter was another staple commodity sold by the shops and later margarine, besides a host of new lines introduced at the start of the new century. By then, of course, Drew was no longer directly involved in the company, which was very effectively run by his relation by marriage, William

Frances Richardson in the garden at Wadhurst. She married Julius Drewe in 1890; painting by Charles Hardie, 1902 (Main Stairs)

Slaughter, a solicitor and the company's chairman for 30 years. Slaughter expanded the firm even more rapidly, so that by 1906 it had over 500 branches. Up to that year Home and Colonial shares usually paid a 15 per cent dividend, and Drew, as the majority shareholder, reaped the benefit. Profits fell abruptly between 1905 and 1911, but after a boardroom row in 1912 the company recovered. He could become a country gentleman without financial qualms.

In 1890 he married Frances Richardson, then described as 'a tall, slender and very beautiful young girl', and the couple set up home in a mock castle, Culverden, a romantic battlemented early nineteenth-century building near Tunbridge Wells in Kent. In the nine years they lived there Frances bore her husband three sons: Adrian, born 1891, a medical research scientist, who was killed in Flanders in 1917 serving in the Royal Garrison Artillery; Basil, born 1894, a barrister, who succeeded his father at Castle Drogo and died in 1974, and Cedric, born 1896, an MP for 29 years, who died in 1971.

In 1899 the family moved to Wadhurst Hall in East Sussex, a vast red-brick mansion built in the 1870s by Edward Tarver for two bachelor brothers, Adrian and Cristobal de Murietta, who were Spanish merchants with interests in South America. A third brother, José, also lived in the house with his Spanish wife, an exceptionally clever and beautiful woman who was a favourite of the Prince of Wales. José was an extravagant socialite whose two daughters married into the aristocracy. The Prince was present at both weddings and was a frequent visitor to Wadhurst, which was renowned for having some of the best shooting in the south of England and was referred to as 'the Princely Estate'. These brilliant years had a sad end. In the 1890s the Argentinians defaulted on bond payments, throwing the financial house of Baring into crisis – and the Muriettas with it. The brothers went spectacularly bankrupt and were thereby forced to sell the house and its entire contents, which explains the presence of the tapestries and exotic Spanish furniture now at Castle Drogo. The move seems to have given Drew respectability within the establishment. In 1900 he became a Sussex JP and by that year was listed in Burke's *Landed Gentry* as 'Drew of Wadhurst Hall',

Wadhurst Hall, East Sussex, where the Drewes lived before the building of Castle Drogo

whereas his partner Musker was not listed; neither were his rivals Lipton, who chose to spend his wealth on yachting and charity work, and Sainsbury, who stayed firmly in his business. This must have given him great satisfaction as he had become absorbed in tracing his family's ancestry – an interest that was to determine the course of his life.

The family's ancestry was respectable. Julius's great-grandfather, Thomas Drew, had practised as a surveyor in London, but according to family tradition his roots were in Devon: a branch of the Drew family were landowners in the east of the county. The Peeks were also a Devon family, from Loddiswell in the south.

Julius had two older brothers. The second of these, William, a barrister, consulted a professional genealogist who suggested to William and Julius that they were descended from the Drewes of Broadhembury near Honiton, whose property had by then passed to the Locke family and was for sale. In 1901 Julius Drew bought part of this property and enlarged a farmhouse to make the present Broadhembury House, in which he installed his brother William. He also changed his name in 1910 by deed poll to the more authentic spelling by adding an 'e' to the end. But that was not all the genealogist revealed. The pedigree contrived to show the family descent from Drogo, the latinised form of Dru, a Norman baron who had accompanied William the Conqueror to England and who was recorded as a landowner in the Devon and Somerset Domesday inventory. His descendant, Drogo de Teigne, gave his name to the parish of Drewsteignton in the twelfth century. By happy coincidence Julius's first cousin, Richard Peek, was rector of Drewsteignton, and Julius had visited him on several occasions. It must have been on these visits that he conceived the idea of building a castle here, on the home ground of his remote ancestor.

CHAPTER SIX

THE BUILDING OF CASTLE DROGO

There were no half-measures about Julius Drewe's enthusiasm for his role as descendant of the Norman baron. He resolved that his castle should not be a theatrical pastiche like Culverden, but a solid granite fortification built on a truly defensive site astride a narrow ridge commanding the Chagford Vale to the north and the River Teign's gorge to the south. Fortuitously this was glebe land belonging to his cousin, the rector of Drewsteignton, which he was able to buy in 1910. Other parcels of land followed, including, in 1921, 250 acres of Whiddon Park on the opposite side of the gorge. This comprised a house built by Sir John Whiddon (died 1575), a prominent Elizabethan lawyer, and his deer-park surrounded by a granite wall of cyclopian proportions. At the time of his death Drewe had amassed an estate of 1,500 acres.

Having acquired the land, Drewe next sought an architect and chose Edwin Lutyens. Why he did so is not certain. Basil Drewe believed his father asked the advice of Edward Hudson, the proprietor of *Country Life*, for whom Lutyens had built Deanery Garden in Berkshire and, more significantly, re-modelled Lindisfarne Castle in Northumberland. Hudson believed Lutyens was 'the only possible architect' and Lindisfarne would have appealed to Drewe for its craggy qualities. He would also almost certainly have known of Lutyens's reputa-

The castle from the west

Perspective sketch by Lutyens of the castle dated 1911, showing the south front with the great hall, which was later abandoned

tion as the designer of numerous houses in Surrey, Sussex and Kent over the previous 20 years, all within a short distance of Wadhurst, and many published in *Country Life*. In any event Drogo had been launched by 3 August 1910, when Lutyens wrote to his wife:

Mr Drew writes a nice and exciting letter to go on with drawings not more than £50,000 though and £10,000 for the garden. I suppose £60,000 sounds a lot to you but I don't know what it means. If I look at Westminster Abbey it is an absurd – trivial amount. If I look at a dear little old world two roomed cottage it merely looks a vast and unmanageable amount. Only I do wish he didn't want a castle – but just a delicious lovable house with plenty of good large rooms in it.

One can understand Lutyens's misgivings over the colossal size of the original project, which would have cost well over £60,000. It was designed on a courtyard plan with three principal rooms flanking the south side: a drawing-room, great hall and dining-room, linked by a vestibule which also acted as the main entrance to the house from within the courtyard. A billiard room and cloisters formed the western wing, joining a chapel to the north, while service quarters filled the east wing and joined a servants' hall which balanced the chapel to the north.

Early sketches of the building favoured an architectural style not dissimilar to Lutyens's Surrey houses, borrowing from the vernacular tradition of Tudor manor houses even to the extent of adding a gabled roof and tall chimneystacks, but not for long. Just over a month after the previous letter Lutyens wrote again to his wife, 'He [Drew] wants to build a large keep or commemorative tower to commemorate the first Drogo and this will be over and beyond the £60,000 castle', and the gables and chimneys disappeared. In their place a castle with genuine defensive characteristics emerged while the Tudor vernacular was recognised only in the freely rendered mullioned windows. A number of sources for a building in this style have been suggested, none more convincing than Flete in south-west Devon, completed in 1881 for the Mildmay family by Norman Shaw, an architect whom Lutyens greatly admired. The ground plan also changed as the courtyard scheme gradually contracted to something more manageable, but not before the site was pegged out in the summer of 1910 by Lutyens and Julius Drewe's eldest son, Adrian.

Christopher Hussey in his biography of Lutyens reflects that April 1911 marked the peak of Lutyens's activities. In addition to the several large houses then in the course of construction, he was

*Castle Drogo under construction in 1913. The vaulted
ceiling of the Kitchen can be seen on the right*

busy completing work on Hampstead Garden
Suburb, preparing a memorial to Edward VII
in Trafalgar Square, designing the British Pavilion
for the Rome Exhibition and the Rand Regi-
ment Memorial in South Africa. This last was one
of several commissions he received from the
Dominion, which he visited at the end of 1910.
The journey presaged others he would make to
India after 1912 to supervise his masterpiece, the
Viceroy's House, but time spent on the long sea
voyages was not wasted. A cabin would be fitted
out as a drawing office and work continued. It is
a curious thought that plans for Castle Drogo,
an English country house deep in Devon, were
drawn to the accompaniment of 'the swash and
roar of the water and a persistent creaking' of an
ocean liner.

Castle Drogo's foundation stone was laid on 4
April 1911, Julius Drewe's 55th birthday. In overall
control was Lutyens himself from his office in

Queen Anne's Gate in London, and in his absence
A. J. Thomas, his office manager. On site was Mr
Drewe's agent, John Walker, whose coordinating
role was crucial throughout. He was a Yorkshireman, trained as a stonemason, who had worked for
the Duke of Portland at Welbeck in Notting-
hamshire before moving to Devon. He lived in
Drewsteignton and every day drove a pony and
trap the three miles to the castle and back. He was
red-haired, irascible, seldom took holidays and was
a stickler for accuracy in everything he did. He was
paid £5 per week. There are over 8,000 copies of
letters he wrote concerning the work. Two extracts
indicate the sort of man he was. Writing to the joinery firm that was fitting panelling in 1915, he
remarked tersely, 'The batons your joiners fixed are
not true by 11/16ths of an inch . . . the remark made
by your manager that half an inch is near enough
does not apply in this case.' Two years previously
he had written to Lewis Bearne, the castle's builder,
'After two minutes past six no man must start
[work] until the half hour and be deducted for it.'

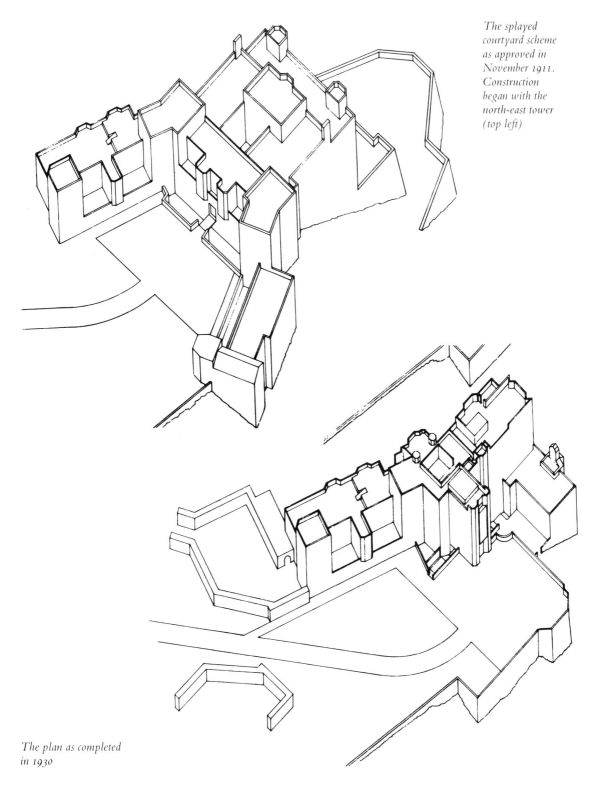

The splayed courtyard scheme as approved in November 1911. Construction began with the north-east tower (top left)

The plan as completed in 1930

The timber mock-up of the barbican in 1913

Bearne's firm was based at Newton Abbot and known locally for completing the Manor House at North Bovey in 1907 for Lord Hambledon. Now under Bearne's direction about 100 men were employed at Castle Drogo at any one time, except during the First World War. Stone-cutters were the backbone of this force, then the labourers, the skilled masons and two or three blacksmiths and carpenters. They worked a 50½-hour week with half an hour off for lunch. In 1914 labourers were paid 8d per hour, the skilled men a little more. Any misbehaviour and they would be given one hour's notice to leave. It was a harsh regime but not unusual for the time. Indeed, Julius Drewe took an interest in the men's welfare by encouraging and supplying equipment for football and cricket, organising summer fêtes and providing provisions at Christmas.

Apart from one minor mishap – Lutyens had forgotten to obtain local planning permission for the castle – progress in the first year was good. Concrete foundations were sunk, outcrops of rock moved and 28,000 trees planted. On one point

Drewe's instructions were clear, the castle should be built in traditional fashion. This meant no cavity walls and no bricks, only solid granite quarried locally at Merivale, Blackinstone and Pew Tor. But even while all this activity went on, the final plan remained undecided.

By the end of 1911 the north wing of the courtyard scheme was abandoned as the west and east wings were splayed, each some 20 degrees off the central axis of the main south block. Then a year later this symmetrical arrangement was halved and for the first time the present plan of two wings joined at an angle of 120 degrees became recognisable, although the great hall along the south front was still retained. Eventually this too disappeared as the castle assumed its final plan with the negligible south front and the chapel fashioned out of the undercroft of the great hall. Not yet decided were the ambitious outbuildings: triangular lodges and a curtain wall and barbican guarding the approach. In the hot summer of 1913, when Walker measured temperatures of 100°F and no rain for nearly three months, timber mock-ups of each were erected for Drewe's inspection. He decided against them, as Walker recorded with some relief in a letter to

Lutyens in October 1913: 'I am pleased to hear that it is now settled what to do to complete the mansion.'

By that time Drewe had taken to renting Kilmorie, a house in Torquay which was used by the family during the summer months, and which he eventually bought. Luggage would be conveyed by Pickford's van from Wadhurst and the family travelled in the Rolls or a Great Western Railway slip coach. Walker meticulously reported progress in a weekly letter and Drewe would visit from time to time. From 1924 onwards he and the family sometimes stayed at the castle or Lutyens would visit his client at Torquay. The Drewe children discovered Lutyens was a 'perfect tease':

He would always have all the peppers and salts and everything at the table arranged as he wanted them to illustrate a point connected with the design and he would make a lot of very quick sketches.

Drewe *père* regarded his architect as a friend, but one not easily swayed from his professional opinions.

An exchange of letters in the autumn of 1912 over Lutyens's revised instructions to the stonemasons shows each had firm opinions. Drewe wrote:

May I ask *why* you have altered your opinion as to preparation of the granite facing? From the commencement you expressed your firm decision that only rough granite should be used. You told Jenkins that no tool marks were to be visible on any piece. He went on with what you told him to do and would have gone on doing so had you been detained at Delhi. To my mind . . . the building should be continued to your pre-Delhian instructions. What might have happened to us if you had also seen the Pyramids as well makes us quake to think about.

Lutyens explained:

The big, lumpy blocks are right for the lower courses but quite impossible to carry them up . . . it will mean a barbaric building worthy of a small municipal corporation. When a barbarian built a fortress he heaped up rocks and his women behind them. If those hard, wide stones are what you think I meant I am the Barbarian! I am very keen about your castle and must 'fight' you when I KNOW I am right.

Julius Drewe (left), Frances Drewe (second left) and their five children at Castle Drogo

Of course, this Edwardian euphoria did not last. By early 1913 rainwater was penetrating the granite, causing a problem that was not eradicated until 1989. In 1914 faults were also found in the asphalt used for waterproofing and the work had to be done again by Italian specialists. The building was also delayed by a continual shortage of worked granite, and in 1914 outbreaks of typhoid in neighbouring villages affected the workforce. These reverses could be overcome, but the outbreak of the First World War had far more devastating effects. Over three-quarters of the men joined the Services and progress was 'fearfully slow'. Then in 1917 Adrian Drewe was killed on active service and, as his sister relates, 'The joy very much went out of life as far as my father and mother were concerned and things were very much quieter and my father really was somewhat of an invalid afterwards.' It says much for Julius Drewe's determination that despite these blows and a three-fold rise in building costs he persevered towards completion of his castle.

In 1919 the Crediton firm of Dart & Francis began to fit mahogany panelling in the day nursery, the start of a twelve-year connection with the castle by the firm. In 1921 a garden was planned along the east front, but moved the following year to its present landscaped site. An especially important date was 22 December 1925, as Albert Thomas observed in a letter to Walker, 'I also note the Last Stone of the Castle proper will be fixed today and the crane taken down; I should say this is "some"

termination to the Year. Congratulations!' The family were able to start living at the house two years later. Unhappily for Julius Drewe his health had suffered further from a stroke in 1924 and he was able to enjoy his new home for only a short time before he died in Torquay in 1931. He was buried in Drewsteignton churchyard beneath a simple granite tomb designed by Lutyens. The pall-bearers included his butler, Mr Rayner, and Messrs Dowdney and Cleave, the two skilled masons who had worked on his castle. His second son, Basil, succeeded him.

Basil Drewe had served with distinction in the Royal Artillery during the First World War, being awarded the MC and Bar. In 1920 he became a barrister specialising in patent law. During the Second World War he joined the RAF and served as a Wing Commander in charge of radar defences, while his mother and his sister Mary ran Castle Drogo, at the family's expense, as a home for babies made homeless by the London Blitz. Shortly after the war Basil Drewe became a Bencher of the Inner Temple and moved back to the castle, where he lived until his death in 1974.

The Drogo estate had been vested in his son Anthony some years previously and he and his wife, Margaret, continued to live in the house on the upper floor of the main block. It is to Anthony Drewe and his son, Dr Christopher Drewe, that the National Trust is indebted for the gift of the house and surrounding land of 600 acres in 1974.

The Library

The portcullis and heraldic Drewe lion on the entrance tower

THE TRUST TAKES OVER

In March 1973 the National Trust received a letter, just one sentence long, from Anthony Drewe at Castle Drogo. 'I write to enquire whether the National Trust would be interested in acquiring this house together with the Teign Gorge stretching over to Fingle Bridge?' No one among the Trust's staff had previously visited the castle which had been the Drewe's home for the last 60 years, but two articles for *Country Life* in 1945 had portrayed enticing images of 'this stark beautiful shimmering building'. Meetings with Mr Drewe were arranged and reports prepared. It was observed, rightly, that, 'no private family would expect to live in the whole house for much longer', but wrongly, 'the castle seems to be in good order other than a small amount of work needed to the roof and some re-pointing'. Estimates for that work suggested £20,000 would be needed to 'put the building in first class order'. Optimistic plans to introduce a special 'Discoval' damp membrane beneath the parapet and £3,000 worth of asphalt on the roof proved ineffectual. Thirty years and one million pounds later, the Trust is still attempting to remedy the roof's deficiencies. There was also doubt that the Castle would attract sufficient visitor numbers. Fifty thousand per annum were anticipated at a charge of 50 pence each. Again, this was a wild miscalculation. Today 120,000 flock annually to the Castle which is the Trust's 4th most popular house in Devon and Cornwall. Since 1975 2,700,000 visitors have travelled to the Castle.

Originally cars were parked on the Castle forecourt and the property was closed during lunchtime. Changes had to be made and visitor facilities built. In May 1974 instructions were issued to a local architect to design a visitor reception building and car park, create the restaurant in the house, organise two staff flats, install new lavatories and bring in mains electricity to replace the turbine-generated power supply. The cost was little more than £16,000. In the same month, the *Daily Telegraph* announced the transfer of ownership from Anthony Drewe to the National Trust. Invitations to the formal handover of the castle to the Trust on 25 March 1975 were issued. The arrangements for the ceremony, as conveyed to Anthony Drewe, were to provide each guest with 'some sort of stirrup cup or punch to keep the cold out' and then for Mr Drewe to hand the castle's keys to the Trust's chairman, Lord Antrim. The party would then go inside for 'proper drinks in the library' and lunch would be served. There followed a tour of the house and 'a cup of tea for those who were still hanging around by 3.30pm'. Happily, the weather was fine and this very understated and English ceremony passed without incident.